What A Woman Wants!

Knowing What Really Satisfies a Woman

La Presha La Valle Mastin

Parson's Porch & Company

What A Woman Wants!

Knowing What Really Satisfies A Woman

Parson's Porch Books

What A Woman Wants! Knowing What Really Satisfies A Woman

ISBN: Softcover 978-0692409718

Copyright © 2015 by La Presha La Valle Mastin

All rights reserved. No part of this book may be reproduced or transmitted in any form or by any means, electronic or mechanical, including photocopying, recording, or by any information storage and retrieval system, without permission in writing from the publisher.

To order additional copies of this book, contact:

Parson's Porch Books
1-423-475-7308
www.parsonsporch.com

Parson's Porch Books is an imprint of Parson's Porch & Company (PP&C) in Cleveland, Tennessee. PP&C is an innovative non-profit organization which raises money by publishing books of noted authors, representing all genres. All donations from contributors and profits from publishing are shared with the poor.

Acknowledgements

To my Lord and Savior Jesus Christ, thank you so much for your love, support, wisdom and patience. Thank You for helping and enlightening me on WHAT A WOMAN WANTS! I will always be willing to help people in need of directions and strength. You are a beacon of LIGHT and thank You for shining in my life! My life belongs to you and my passion is to be aware that you are constantly guiding and using me to make a difference in the lives of your people. I dedicate everything I do to you! You alone get the glory! I am available to assist in every way I can that your glory will be revealed and people will be blessed through you! I love you very much!

To my precious mother, Mother Mae Mastin! You are a jewel and such a perfect role model! I love you very much. Thank you for your support, patience, wisdom, kindness, love, and encouragement! You have helped me in many ways; your strength; your poise; your beauty and your talents allows me to be who I am today; you have encouraged me not to allow what people say or do to hinder me from moving forward! I will always appreciate and love you! You are the best mother and friend I could ever asked for, I thank God for you! Stay blessed!

To my family and close friends, you are so dear to me words cannot express how much I appreciate you. You have been very instrumental to me! You have inspired me to be the best I can be, to utilize my gifts and to always give God the glory! Thank you so much for your support, love, encouragement, patience, wisdom, time and kindness you have given me. You are the best!

Many thanks to my grandmother, La Valle Warren and my father, Steger J. Mastin Jr., Glenda Williams, John Churn, Angela Jordan, Evangelist Stephanie Boyd-Campbell, Prophetess LaCrissa M. Bird, Francille Fortson, Juanita Fells, Joyce Henderson, Carolyn Lockhart, Darlene Williams, Supervisor, Mother Dianne Bogan, Pastor Marquaello Futrell, Lady Kanesha Futrell, Dr. T. Marie Brown, Dr. Elijah Hankerson, Lady Rachel Hankerson, Dr. Rita Womack, Dr. Rosella Burks, Mother Theresa E. Bolden, Lance Austin, Steger J. Mastin III, Katherine Mastin, Kanbreale Mastin, LaWanda Mastin, Mother Orpha Schell, Bishop R.J. Ward, Mother Dorothy Ward, Pastor Robert C. and First Lady Catherine Williams, GaRita Warren, Beverly White, Robert Warren, Mary Alice Warren, Ronald Warren, Mary Warren, District Missionary Gloria Cunningham, District Missionary Josephine Boyd, Mother Bertha McDonald, Peggy Rush-White, Supervisor, Mother Mary Tucker, Denice Roach, Prophetess Janice Mixon, Pastor William Foster, First Lady Kenya Foster, Dell M. Brown, Brenda Baker-Lee, Lady Shirley Wooten, Edgar Samuel, John Michael Richardson, Aunt Creasie White, Andrea White-Griffin, Vinzella Newson, Charlene Gaines, Trudy Anderson, Jo Travaglini, Susan Rabbitt, Constance Ivy, Elesha Broyles, Katrina Broyles, Mother Sular Gordon, Evangelist Yvonne Martin, Howard (Dalllas) Jamison III, Lady Angela Sanders, Sandra Southerland, Sabra Moore, Prophet Rodney Reveling, LaVern Carter and Danielle Frazier, Reverend, Dr. Ronald Bobo, Sr., and Rev. Dr. David Russell Tullock.

THANK YOU SO MUCH!

Table of Contents

Introduction *The Man I Love So Much!!!*	9
Wisdom *Hear The Empowering Voices of Great Men and Women Worldwide!*	11
What A Woman Wants *Knowing What Really Satisfies A Woman*	19
A Woman Wants To Be Loved *Passions From The Heart!*	25
A Woman Wants To Be Appreciated *You Are Important To Me!*	35
A Woman Wants To Be Accepted *Loving Me For Who I Am!*	43
A Woman Wants Affections *You Mean The World To Me!*	57
A Woman Wants To Be Respected *Honored! I Will Do All I Can Not To Hurt You!*	65
A Woman Wants Trust *The Untold Secrets!*	75
A Woman Wants Security *Safety!!! Whew!*	83

Introduction
The Man I Love So Much!!!

As I reflected over my life, I can truly say that I've been blessed to have had a great, amazing, loving, funny, hardworking, great provider and faithful daddy and father, Steger John Mastin Jr.! My daddy loved me unconditional! I was his little girl. He treated me like a princess nothing was too good for me or too much for me; whenever I wanted something my daddy always provided the things I needed and wanted. And I wasn't a spoil brat. He loved his family so much and he showed his love daily to us. Fond memories flood my soul! He was my protector! My encourager! My supporter! My hero!!!! My daddy was my everything!!!!! As I write this, I can't help but cry because I miss him dearly! I looked like my father! I honored my daddy! I respected my daddy! Daily, I showed my daddy how much I loved him and appreciated him! I was proud to let people know he was my father! He was a well-dressed man! He was overwhelming handsome! He was tall and very distinguished gentleman! He was very mannerable, helpful, giving, caring, supportive, kind, and he stood for a needy cause, and he was a tall and distinguished gentleman! He didn't entertain negative people; he stay focused on his passions and accomplished everything he set out to do! I have a lot of his special characteristics in me.

My father taught me at a young age to becoming an adult, how a man should treat me! What to accept and what not to accept. My father taught me well! My father knew another man's character. I'm very selective when it comes to marriage! I know and expect a man should treat me with the upmost respect! He should value my thoughts and feelings! He should honor me as the lady I am!

Steger John Mastin Jr! (my daddy), you are my solid rock! I pray the man I marry will have the same characteristics you had! Thank you for all you have done to help make me the woman I am today! I cherish you in my heart! Your love, kindness, support and laughter will always make me smile! You are the GREATEST! I thank God for allowing you to be my daddy and for me to be your daughter! We were two peas in a pod! We were inseparable! I love you forever!

Your Little Girl,

La Presha

Wisdom

Hear The Empowering Voices of Great Men and Women Worldwide!

Ladies First! What happened to the respect? For women today in our society, did you forget us? Are you using us for our goods, treating us like we don't matter? Even though we are a part of God's creation. What happened to the respect? We are leaders! We are not to be disrespect! A strong woman wears the look of confidence on her face and she wears grace. Put ladies first! Without women there wouldn't be reproduction and new generation! I'm talking to the women who ever been hunted down, killed off because of sexual predators! I'm talking to the women who ever lost a child! Women, it's time to line up for battle! It's time to march for respect! It's time to demand a change! It's time to show dominance! It's time to put ourselves first! And be leaders to the little girls showing them it's not good to do drugs and it's not good to sell your bodies! We are not known for that, but we are known as leaders! Show loyalty to another! A woman of strength has faith; it is in the journey that she will become strong! Ladies First!

-GaNaee Warren

As you travel in life and become successful, don't forget to reach back and help someone else to succeed.

-Mae Mastin

Women, we should get what we need so that we can help others get what they need…Reaching out to others helps you broaden your experiences, learn more about yourself and also gain a wonderful sense of pride!

-Angela Jordan

Just remember that no one and nothing can compete with favor when it's God's favor that rests on your life

-Elesha Broyles

A curse is a blessing blocker!! Live differently! Be different! Do something different for yourself and others! Then you will make a difference!

-Dell Marie Brown

Always remember, a person's life never resembles the "Now Showing" poster you see. We're humans, we're not perfect and we're going to make mistakes. You can't photoshop your life. Be willing to improve on the photo negatives…I'm just saying (ijs)

-Howard (Dalllas) Jamison III

We have to be the better person. The way the world is today we need to keep our love one close by being kind to the ones who are reaching out for love, kindness and understanding and they haven't learned how to except it for their own reasons. If you can keep an open mind and loving heart God will continue on blessing you. Speaking from experience.

-Peggy Rush-White

No matter what has happened in the past, it does not detract from your value. God still wants to use you. You were not broken to become useless, rather to be opened to more of His power, love and grace. You have what the world needs to be blessed. Encourage your sister with your testimony. Strengthen your friends with your words. God's perfect plan for you has begun. "For I know the plans I have for you, declares the Lord, plans to prosper you and not harm you, plans to give you hope and a future." This is your season of change. Mediocre to excellence; just enough to abundance; depression to joy; drug abuse to freedom; hurt to forgiveness; and from the back to the front. GOD WANTS YOU!

-Elder Rodney M. Reavling, Sr.

Philippians 4:13 says, "I can do all things through Christ Jesus that strengthens me." This is one of my favorite scriptures. I was told there would be things I could never do with God on my side all things are possible…Be blessed…

-Sandra Southerland

Live so God can use you anywhere and anytime. Stay ready……..keep a now word in your mouth; A word of edification, exhortation and comfort; to build up and never to tear down. This is the will of the Father concerning us.

-Mother Sular Gordon

In all that you say, in everything you do; stay prayerful. Keep God first and everything will fall in the right place at the right time.

-Juanita Fells

Know that God is our everything! Pray. When we pray to God we can be sure that He hears us and will answer our prayers. John 17:9-20; James 5:13-18

-Evangelist Yvonne Martin

Women of excellence! Wait on the Lord….What's in the W-A-I-T? Wisdom: Christ is the key that opens the hidden treasures of God's wisdom. Keep studying the Word! Anointing: You are anointed for "service in God's kingdom. Keep "fasting and praying" in the spirit of consecration. Intercession: The Holy Ghost helps you to intercede for others while God is working on your behalf. Keep looking up. Temperance: Self-control and self-discipline are exemplary characteristics of true believers. Keep it ALL under control. Absolute Joy Today!

-Lady Angela Sanders

I am what I am and where I am because of the positioning of God in my life! Seeking God involves fasting, praying, studying His word and developing an intimate relationship with Him. Seeking God will bring you to a place where you not only know His voice, but you are CLOSE ENOUGH to hear His voice when He speaks. It will bring you to a place where you not only hear His voice, but OBEY his voice... becoming one with Him and taking on the mind of Christ Jesus. Seek ye first the kingdom of God until His will and your will become one and it's no more I, but the Christ that lives in me and until I only desire what He desires for me. And all these things shall be added unto you. Matthew 6:33. "These things" that you have need of or desire will follow you seeking God. God wants to be first in our lives and it is His good pleasure to give us the desires of our heart. Many ladies seek things and people...which is the reverse of God's plan for success.

-Lady Shirley Wooten

God's bounty is limited only by us, not by His resources, power or willingness to give. Jabez was blessed simply because he refused to let any obstacle, person or opinion loom larger than God's nature. And God's nature is to bless. His kindness in recording Jabez's story in the Bible is proof that it's not who you are or what your parents decided for you or what you were "fated" to be that counts. What counts is knowing who you want to be and asking for it. Through a simple, believing prayer, you can change your future. You can change what happens one minute from now.

-Edgar Samuel

A woman of God should have a close relationship with God. It's not enough just to know Him, but let Him be Lord of your life. That's where He has complete control of your life. Love Him with all your heart, soul and mind; build your faith in Him and trust Him. Keep a prayer life daily and seek Him for guidance in every situation. Set future goals for your life and keep them. Remember, the sky is limitless to what you can have.

-LaVern Carter

When we acknowledge God in all our ways, He equips us for the Journey!

-Evangelist Darlene Williams

To a woman of God who will and has undoubtedly made an impact on people everywhere across the world, this is just the beginning of the miracles, signs and wonders that is set before you!

-Katrina Broyles

To all the women reading this book, let me encourage you. When things get tough and you've tried everything you can think of. Try Jesus, for He is the answer to all your problems. All you have to do is trust Him for He will bring you out alright. Take care and be abundantly blessed!

-Evangelist Brenda Baker-Lee

We are simple, yet complicated creatures according to man. But God says, "He will give us the desires of our hearts" when you commit to Him. What a Woman wants is simple, yet complicated-but in some cases just the basic things in life is so meaningful; a strong relationship, financial stability and a spiritual enlightenment. I know through experiences of daily prayer, setting goals and staying focus, a woman will get what she wants to fulfill her dreams and hopes. Make sure that what you say is really what you want. Challenge yourself to want more in life, you may just surprise others in who you really are.

-Evangelist Constance Ivy

Your energy, joy and peace will eventually die if your only ambition in life is to please man. However, when you aim to please God, somehow, your energy has a tendency of being renewed, your joy strengthened and your peace would pass all understanding. Many times, God will give His people a glimpse at their destiny, but it's up to the people to follow His road map to the finish line.

-Evangelist Rachel Hankerson

What A Woman Wants
Knowing What Really Satisfies A Woman

The REAL You! Did you know you are a phenomenal woman! From the moment of conception through your infancy, through being a toddler, pre-teen, teenager to an adult; you have amazing characteristics that makes you unique. Phenomenal, you are! No one can do what you can do! You are the glue that keeps things together! You are the one that helps this universe evolve! You are the one to help bring peace to an unrest soul! Phenomenal! Phenomenal! That's who you are!

A woman is a female adult and she has a very important role; for centuries, women have been the backbone for their family, standing for justice for fair labor and withstanding the criticism from the oppressor, yet rising to be the great woman she is and undoubtedly able to accomplish her dreams and visions for herself and her family.

Being a woman, I understand what a lot of women want; by listening to her purpose, her visions, her aspirations and her hurts, I got a sense of her passion! It isn't difficult to tap into the sincerity of a woman, though at times it's a mystery, but it's a woman's desires to be treated with total respect. The purpose of this book is to bring awareness and to empower readers, to know who women were created to be and have the ability to tap into the feelings, thoughts and emotions of a woman; her needs, her desires and her wants. She is a lady who speaks and walks in a polite manner, well-respected and confident, she doesn't lower her standards; she is gentle, kind, graceful and determined to live her life to the fullness. However, a woman has needs and desires. What a woman wants is compassion, a listening ear, kindness, support, flowers, candy, thank you (word of mouth, or a card) and to hear the words "I love you" and "I appreciate you".

A woman is feminine! Soft-spoken, gentle and kind! Yet, she has the ability to ward off perpetrators, who try to hurt her family! She has the ability to spot out villains from afar off! She can sense when something is wrong! She strategically knows how to protect herself and her family without breaking a heel or pulling off her earrings or greasing her face with Vaseline! Yes, she is a SUPERWOMAN! She has the power and strength to make sure her family is safe! In the life of a woman and all she does! She successfully manages to bring harmony to what could be a stressful day and sometimes it is! A woman's strength and commitment allows her to oversee daily duties that bring balance for herself and her entire family. Women are givers by nature of their time, money, affection and strength (physically and emotionally) 24 hours a day, 7 days a week; 365 days in a year nonstop. We are creative, innovative, strong, loyal and dependable, we make things happen! We are the queens in our household and sometimes the king. We persevere doing challenging tasks and overcome them victoriously! We were fashioned (designed) to be unique, beautiful, wealth builders, help meet to our husband, kind, understanding and giving. Women are entrepreneurs, homemakers and career builders. We are emotional beings; we are nurturers full of love and compassion. We make sure everything and everyone is well taken care of meeting the needs and satisfying the wants. And sometimes, we leave our needs and wants last or unfulfilled.

In this powerful book, there are 7 areas of what a woman wants. A woman wants to be: 1) Loved; 2) Appreciated; 3) Accepted; 4) Affection; 5) Respect; 6) Trust and 7) Security. These seven areas are very important and they are associated to a woman's needs and desires.

Depending on the person, some people take these special women for granted. There are women who don't know their self-worth and self-value. Women, we have to come together and develop a positive support system that will help enlighten and empower women all over the world and stop the madness of allowing their feelings to continue to be overlooked and hurt from people they are in some type of relationship with, whether it's their husband, boyfriend, friend or family member and help them to tap into their creative being, their uniqueness and their awesomeness. We are able to affect our environment and promote change to help make a difference in our community, society and the world. You are great and there is no one like you! Don't allow people to take advantage of you. YOU ARE AN AWESOME WOMAN!!!

I am here to help you overcome every obstacles, hindrances and setbacks that has kept you feeling less than who you are. No longer will you be stuck in relationships that will only bring out the worst in you; no longer will you feel sad, lonely and isolated from people; no longer will you struggle trying to let go of the hurts. No longer will you be a doormat letting people walk over you. You were fearfully and wonderfully made. Accomplish your dreams, fulfill your visions and live your best life now! It's nothing wrong for a woman to desire love, appreciation, acceptance, affection, respect, trust and security. Make sure it's from people who are willing and able to provide the things you desire. If not, don't waste your valuable time, move forward!

Phenomenal! That's Who You Are!!!!!

Are You Ready?

Then My Friend Let The Enlightenment And Empowerment Begin!

-La Presha L. Mastin

LOVED!

Passions from the Heart!

*Loved, Adored, Beloved, Cherished,
Precious, Admired, Adoration, Devoted,
Fondness, Tenderness, Yearning, Zeal,
Regarded, Passion, Unity, Friendship,
Honored, Thoughtfulness, Affection*

A Woman Wants To Be Loved! Passions From The Heart!

Every woman would like to experience how it feels to be genuinely loved. Love encompasses a lot of self-sacrificing. According to Webster's dictionary, love simply means to be held in deep affection, to cherish and adore. In today's society, the words, "I love you" is hardly heard. Those three little, but powerful word has great meaning. Love comes from the heart and it reaches the hearts of other people, in addition, to be loved, you must love yourself first before you can love other people. It's very important that you learn how to love yourself. By loving yourself, you must accept yourself for who you are, accept your likes and dislikes; be happy that you are alive and well and value your sense of style, beauty and importance. Loving yourself, help set the standards of how you want other people to love you in return. Loving someone isn't automatically given. You have to have some kind of understanding with that person, it has to be communicated and understood in order for two or more people to establish affections that connect them emotionally, physically and mentally with another person(s). When it comes to love, you don't always have the answers, ask questions and don't assume. You should tell people how to love you in the way you want to be loved. There are standards you can establish how you want to be loved: 1) knowing who you are; 2) knowing what you want; 3) not settling for second best and 4) not complicating your life with complicating people. People who love you will go above and beyond to help make you happy; when there is a need, they will try to help you without you asking for their help, there are no limits to what they will do for you.

From the beginning of creation, there are people who are exhibiting conditional love which is called phileo love. Phileo love is a fleshly and self-centered love. It is based on human feelings which are unstable with high and low emotions. This type of love looks out for personal gain and it entraps people to do want he/she wants, need and desires. In essence, people with this type of love says, "if you love me then, I love you; if you help me then, I will help you and/or if you treat me bad then, I will treat you bad, or if you treat me good then, I will treat you good." This is the worst type of love, really it isn't love at all; it's full of emotions, personal gain, control and trickery. Phileo love doesn't last long, it's temporary and you will find people in and out of relationships and at the end all they have left are baggage of hurts, disappointments and regrets. In the end, a person will lose out on what love really is and how it feels when he/she exhibits phileo love. People define and display love in different ways; when you are in a relationship, it's very important to know what he/she likes and dislikes; you want them to enhance your life not deplete it.

Genuine love never seeks to harm another person; rather love seeks peace, patience, forgiveness, understanding, kindness, wisdom and compassion for the person you love. Genuine love oozes out of one person to another person daily for the rest of their lives. Unconditional love which is called agape love is a selfless love; it considers people's happiness, its understanding and kind. Agape love is heartfelt and it's considerate and it put the concerns of people before itself, it's limitless and it's perfect. Agape love says, "I'll do anything for you to help make you happy because it's in my heart to do, whether it's reciprocated or not, just because I love you." It's putting someone else's needs, desires and wants before your own. Love is sharing and caring with the one you love. Spending quality time with that special person; sometimes, it's walking in the mall or the park holding hands; running errands; pulling out a chair; opening and closing doors; assisting with her coat; foot massages; back rubs; breakfast in bed; a kind word and a listening ear. Love is longevity and fruitful. These things speak volume to a woman!

Key Words to Consider:

Affection

Affection comes when someone dear to you has made a lasting imprint or impression in your life. The mere thought of that person; their smile, their fragrant smell, their kindness, their support and their encouraging word(s) leaves a warm feeling in your heart of gratitude that will last throughout eternity. You will never forget how much you adore and admire their qualities and the unity that brought you together; you will never forget how much you appreciate their endless patience and faithfulness during challenging moments and the love you have in your heart, no one could ever replace; they will forever be in your heart whether present or absence. Affection says, "You are important to me! I think of you often and you make me smile! You matter to me! And I appreciate you!"

Some point in our lives, we have met people who have said the right things, who have done the right things and who have given their time and energy to support and encourage us when we needed it. At times, misunderstandings in a relationship take place and separation occurs, but the kindness shown and given will never be erased or go unnoticed when that person has left a lovely impression in your heart. Wow! That's deep!

Cherish

Cherish every moment you have with the one you love. Never take people for granted! People are in your life for a purpose and they help bring out the best in you; also, they help you fulfill your goals, dreams and visions. Fond memories of happiness, joy and love are priceless! Fond memories of laughter and celebrations of joyous occasions you shared together. Cherish the very present with the one you love, don't take them for granted. Give to them the love they need and they will automatically give you the love you need. Don't be afraid to love; open your heart to people who are genuine, kind, giving, supportive, encouraging and loveable. They will not hurt you, disrespect you, offend you or belittle you. Everyone isn't perfect, but love is perfect!

Cherish the person you love interests and their attributes! It's important you have fond memories while doing things together! The person you love may enjoy fishing, but you squirm of the thought of putting worms on a fishing hook or the flies and mosquitoes may be pestering you, go, but allow him to bait your hook or watch him fish, make sure you take some bug spray to ward off the bugs; they may want to go mountain climbing, but you are afraid of heights, go, but wait at the bottom of the mountain; they may enjoy playing golf or watching sports on television or in person at an arena, whatever you do together enjoy and cherish the moment, enjoy yourself; take pictures and later reminiscent over the fun times you shared together. You will never forget the moments you experienced together, you can tell stories to your children, grandchildren and friends. That's Priceless!

Adore

Adore the person you love the way he/she is don't try to change them to be the way you want them to be! Adore their style, their sense of humor, their creative being, their loyalty and their uniqueness. There are people who are worth loving; adore that person and they will adore you. Everyone in this world, doesn't look the same nor act the same. When you adore the person you love, you are saying, "I admire you; I appreciate you; I esteem you and I love you just for being you."

Adore the way they do things to help make you smile; adore the way they say things to brighten your day; and adore the way they support you that help make your day less stressful. It doesn't require a lot of time, money or energy, when it comes from the heart; it's effortless!

It's rewarding! It's not frustrating or demanding, it flows freely when you give it genuinely to the person that you love dearly. To realize you have someone who completes you, who loves you, who adores you and who admires you; wow! That will inform that person they are truly loved!

Love is a beautiful feeling. Love develops an attachment from one person to another. It help affirms the outcome you desire with the one you love. Love is accepting people in spite of their flaws and issues. Love is giving and not looking for anything in return. It's supportive, encouraging; lasting from eternity to eternity. Love endures long and is patient and kind; love never envious nor boils over with jealousy, it's not boastful or vainglorious; it does not display itself haughtily. It is not conceited (arrogant and inflated with pride); it's not rude (unmannerly) and does not act unbecomingly. Love does not insist on its own rights or its own way, for it is not self-seeking; it is not touchy or fretful or resentful; it takes no account of the evil done to it (it pays no attention to a suffered wrong). It does not rejoice at injustice and unrighteousness, but rejoices when right and truth prevail. Love bears up under anything and everything that comes, it is ever ready to believe the best of every person, it hopes are fadeless under all circumstances and endures everything (without weakening). Love never fails (never fades out or become obsolete or come to an end). Embrace love unconditionally and wholeheartedly!

Love and celebrate your strengths, your identity, your uniqueness and your charisma. Recognize your skills, abilities and talents and use them. You are beautiful, smart and special not only to you, but also to others. You must know that you are important, you are valuable, you are gifted and you are needed somewhere in this universe. You are daily loaded with benefits! You have so much to give and so much to do. What you need to do is love on yourself, think positive about yourself, square your shoulders back and hold your head up high and love every ounce of your being because YOU ARE SOMEBODY!   AND YOU ARE LOVED!

Love makes the world go around! Love is contagious! Love is needed to develop and maintain relationships! Love eradicates fear! Love overshadows failure! Love brings peace! Love keeps on growing and glowing! Love enables you to embrace change! Love develops a "can do" attitude! Love brings victory not defeat! Love says we are strong together, not apart! Love covers a multitude of sins! Love never fails! Love endures struggles! Love is present and not absent! Love keeps its word! Love is not cheap! Love is fair! Love is patience! Love says "I'm sorry" to bring peace, even when it wasn't your fault! Love provides quality time, money and support! Love is reframing from hurting someone's feelings! Love is considerate! Love brings out the best in you! Love is full of passion! Love is hope! Love is giving! Love endures forever and ever and ever! Love is Endless!

Love!
Passions From The Heart! Reaches The Heart!
Embrace Love Daily!

APPRECIATED!

You Are Important To Me!

*Grateful, Thankful, Acknowledged,
Indebted, Obligated, Sincere, Gratitude,
Support, Replenished, Restored,
Entitlement, Giver, Selfless, Sacrificing,
Kindness, Loved, Caring, Thoughtfulness,
Gentled, Appreciated, Everlasting*

A Woman Wants To Be Appreciated!
You Are Important To Me!

Every woman would like to be appreciated. How well are you being appreciated? Are you giving more than you are receiving? Do you feel depleted and frustrated? Then check your motives, why are you giving to people who are only receiving and not replenishing you. Their needs and wants are more important than yours. Do you find yourself in the middle or down on their priority list? What type of relationship do you have with this person(s)? Are they worth missing out on enjoying your life, fulfilling your goals and accomplishing your dreams and visions? No, they are not!

Being appreciated is knowing and showing how grateful a person is for kindness that was shown to them. It could be a thank you note or a smile or a helpful hand. According to Webster's dictionary, to be appreciated simply means to be valued or regard highly; place a high esteem; to be grateful or thankful for.

A woman wants to know that she matters, she is not an after-thought or overlooked, she wants her presence known and appreciated. She isn't vulnerable, but she wants to be considered and treated fairly. When a woman constantly gives, gives and gives she need to be replenished, she doesn't have low self-esteem, she know who she is and her self-worth, but she gets tired and drained because she has given out to everybody that is important to her. Some women find other things to do to fulfill their void or to have a sense of entitlement to feel appreciated.

Within a 24 hour day, a woman's job is never ending! She is a mother, wife, daughter, aunt, friend and church member; she is involved in community service(s) helping the needy or a cause to promote change; meeting everybody's needs isn't easy, but it has to be done. She is a homemaker and career-builder; she is active in PTA meetings at her child's school, her child has extra-curricular activities after school and assisting her child with homework; she prepare meals and clean the house and gives her child a bath daily. And it starts all over the following day.

Appreciating the woman you love; sometimes, she would like a "me-moment" a nice place in the house that's secluded, cozy and serene; the atmosphere is peaceful and calming where she can unwind and regroup from her hectic day. In a household the duties are endless! The woman is the "go to" person if someone is missing a sock or shoe; she is the "go to" person when her husband need a button sewn on his shirt; she is the "go to" person when food is lacking in the home and need to go to the grocery store and if house cleaning duties are lacking in the home, she is the "go do it" person. Sometimes, a woman would like help with bathing and feeding the kids, doing the laundry, washing the dishes, cleaning the house, taking out the trash, mowing the grass, raking the leaves, shoveling the snow, grocery shopping, washing her car and filling her gas tank up with gas. Just because she can do these things and sometimes she does it without complaining, please acknowledge and assist her; she is a very valuable part in your household and she help keep and hold things together. Give her a "me-moment" time, she may come home stressed from her day and need to relax and unwind, please give her that time, she needs it. Please!

Celebrate and compliment her when she does a great job preparing meals! Celebrate and compliment her on how well she takes care of the kids! Celebrate and compliment her on providing monetary funds to help support the home! Celebrate and compliment her on how well she takes care of the home! Celebrate and compliment her on how beautiful she looks! Celebrate and compliment her on how wonderful she smells! Celebrate and compliment her because she is the queen of your home! A king needs the queen! (Smile)

A woman wants to be treated like a queen. In a royal family, a queen simply takes her royal position and she is honored and respected and held in high regards by people around her. A queen doesn't conduct or treat herself like a peasant. She carries herself with grace, beauty and charisma. She is adored and well admired by her surroundings. A queen is graced with people who will help make her life easier! She is assisted in her home and she is assisted outside her home! She is treated with royalty! She is appreciated because she is the queen!

A woman likes to look good! She likes to smell good! Her appearance speaks confidence! It is a woman's prerogative to appreciate the finer things in life! A woman like clothes, jewelry, money, manicure and pedicure, perfume and massages; sometimes, she would like to dine at a 5-star restaurant with white linen tablecloths, white linen napkins, stem crystal glassware, china plates, soft music played at her table or in the restaurant, server in a black suit with a black bow tie or black tie around his/her neck with a white linen cloth draped over the left arm. Some women like to dine at a least expensive restaurant which is great; whether it's expensive or least expensive, she desires to be treated like the queen she was created to be. When she looks and feels good, you look and feel good! She is your queen!

Men, I know you have a very busy schedule; attending one business meeting after another or working endless hours at work or working two jobs to support your family. You're a supportive father and husband! A great provider for your family, but on your list of "to do"; please try to make some time to spend with her and please don't make her last on your list of priority! Putting her first, will bring happiness, peace and love into your relationship. She doesn't have a problem giving of her time, energy, support and endless love, but she must know that she is important and appreciated also.

Key Words to Consider:

Value

A woman's value is priceless! She is worth more than a Mona Lisa painting hanging on the wall! She is worth more than an expensive Bentley or Lamborghini or Aston Martin car safely and securely parked in the garage! She is worth more than all the money exchanged on Wall Street! Her value should be noted and appreciated! Value her wit, her classiness, her abilities to be successful in the things she does; value her loyalty and integrity. I stated in the introduction that women are creative, innovative, strong, loyal and dependable, they make things happen! Women were fashioned (designed) to be unique, beautiful, wealth builders, help meet to their husband; they are kind, understanding and giving. These gifts weren't something she pulled out of the sky, but she was born with these special abilities to be amazing, unique, and successful and produce positive change for herself and in the lives of people around her. Her value is priceless! Very rare!

High-Esteem

High-esteem is not a word that produces conceited and stuffy people. It is a word that speaks of a woman's integrity, her value and her respect. A woman with high-esteem; know her character, she know her worthiness, she know her intellect and she know her purpose. A woman with high-esteem walks with confidence! She talks with empowering words helping people to be the best! She gives her love and compassion! She doesn't walk or talk while looking down on someone else; rather she helps that individual(s) in areas they are lacking. She develops resource programs to help educate people who are in need. She stands up for injustice to ensure that other women are treated with dignity and respect! A woman with high-esteem, reach out and lift the next woman up and encourage her not to give up because a change will come. High-esteem is who you are and what you do for yourself and others!

Thankful

Every day take a moment to share how thankful you are for the things she says and does to help make you and your family a place to call home! Share with her the countless blessings of having her in your life! A woman is thankful when a person gives her their time, energy, support, love and respect. People don't have to give another person anything, but when they do the recipient is thankful. Thank you goes a long way when kindness has been given. Send that person a thank you card, a text message or email expressing your gratitude and never forget them; pray for them, be there for them and encourage them. We need one another and we should always be thankful and grateful for special people who are in our lives. When a person appreciates a woman through words or deeds she will never forget you. She will always remember your kindness. If you show her that you appreciate her for who she is, not what she does or does not have, watch your life be full of joy, success and love.

Let Her Know That "You Are Important To Me!"

ACCEPTED!

Loving Me For Who I Am!

Acknowledged, Chosen, Normal, Popular, Preferred, Received, Recognized, Welcomed, Unique, Confident, Belong To, Ordinary, Original, Accepted

A Woman Wants To Be Accepted!
Loving Me For Who I Am!

> *"I am a loveable, unique, valuable, talented and a worthy woman, who is qualified to accomplish my goals and reap wealth and success and receive all of life rewards."*

Every woman wants to be accepted. Accepting who you are allows people to accept you! Webster's dictionary defines accepted as acknowledged, chosen and received. Women are awesome human beings! A lot of us know what we want and what we don't want. When you know who you are and what you want out of life and you convey it to other people it will inform them that you will only be enhanced and not depleted. It says that I love me the way that I am! Always be yourself! Being accepted is not predicated on whose social group you are connected with, it's not being affiliated with a certain class of people and it's not rubbing elbows with people who can open a door of opportunity for you. Acceptance is how you feel about yourself and not how others feel about you. People's opinions should not define who you are! You are not looking for approval from other people to make you feel accepted. You are already unique and fabulous!

Women, surround yourself with people who will speak words of encouragement, love and support to you. Avoid people who criticize your style, your beauty, your accomplishments and your integrity. A woman wants to be loved, she wants to be accepted and she wants to be happy, productive and successful. Please, don't label her or put her in a category, but celebrate her greatness. She may not be who you want her to be, but accept her individuality, don't try to change her to fit your standards because she is the best she was created to be for the person who accepts and appreciates her uniqueness!

My beloved grandmother, LaValle Warren, who was such a wise woman said, "Women have to present themselves in a very respectable way. The way we dress, the way we act or conduct ourselves and the way we talk; we have to speak appropriately in a way that what we say is received and not discarded, dress appropriately that we look like ladies reframing from showing body parts that should only be seen by our husbands; and to walk up straight with our head up and know where we are going in life." Words of wisdom and strength! I love her! Thanks Grandma Val! I am because of you!

Your attitude determines your altitude! And your altitude determines how long you stay ahead! A woman cannot afford to allow her imperfections and insecurities dictate who she is as a person; those feelings will make you not love and appreciate the dynamic person that you are, admiring someone else and hoping you look like that person will not help you. When you develop an attitude of acceptance and self-supporting of yourself and others then you can appreciate your true identity. Stop judging and criticizing your inward and outward appearances because it will leave you emotionally damaged. When you feel bad about yourself, it will result in a lack of confidence, hopelessness, and feelings of being unloved, not appreciated, unattractiveness, loneliness and bad relationships. A woman that accepts her dynamic being is able to focus on her strengths and her weaknesses and take the responsibility to eradicate imperfections and insecurities that lay dormant within her heart and she empowers herself to be the best she can be and never allow flaws and issues to hinder her success. Love and care about yourself! You must appreciate who you are! No one will ever look like you or talk like you or act like you! Never!

You were created uniquely! Divine! Every woman doesn't look like another woman. Every woman's features are beautiful; her eyes, her nose, her hair, her skin tone, her body structure, her style, her poise and her dialect.

Every woman has outstanding abilities to design, to lead, to build and to sustain. Her uniqueness is captivating, well recognized and accepted! When she steps into a room, her persona draws attention and she hasn't said a word, eyes follow her as she grace the room. When she leaves the room, there is a sweet aroma of her presence that remains or lingers in the room. When a person talks to this unique woman, they are left speechless or intrigue with her conversation. The way she carries herself is to be admired by many, she is not trying to prove who she is because she is aware of her identity, her self-worth and her value; she is not trying to fit in where she is not wanted because she recognizes she is in a class all by herself, this unique woman is confident, she accepts and love the person she has become.

A woman that accepts her uniqueness is able to compliment another woman's style and celebrate her accomplishments. She is not inferior to another woman's beauty or success! She's not trying to imitate, compete or belittle another woman. She acknowledges, love and accepts her awesomeness!

Build a woman up with words of encouragement, kindness and love and she will build you up; support her ideas, goals, dreams, visions and aspiration and she will support you; encourage her to move forward and not allow anything or anyone to hinder her purpose and she will always be the woman that makes you happy and fulfilled in your life. What you make happen for her, she will definitely make happen for you.

Key Words to Consider:

Acknowledge

Women have several gifts and abilities! They are creative beings! They know how to prepare and serve great meals; they are skilled fashion designers: purchasing, sewing and designing materials to make a coat, dress, shirt, skirt, pants and blouse! They are crafty jewelry designers! They are chefs, restaurants owners and servers! They are entrepreneurs overseeing adult and child daycare centers, hair care businesses and cosmetics franchises and cakes and cookies businesses! They are CEOs at major corporations. Women are great money handlers and homemakers. They are awesome wives and mothers. When a person has an awesome woman like this in their life, she should be acknowledged and celebrated because she helps stabilize every aspects of life that brings balance and success to the person(s) associated with her. A mere thank you, flowers, vacation or a night off from daily duties will show how much you appreciate her for all she does for you and the family.

Chosen

Wonder why you have so many obligations and deadlines to meet and to complete is because you have been chosen! You have been chosen to help bring success to the needs of others. People can see your greatness, your gifts and your tenacity and because you do such a terrific job in holding down and accomplishing every assigned tasks, people know they can call on you and not worry if the task will be completed successfully. Being chosen initially feels great, when people know they can count on you to get the job done, but sometimes, the tasks can be exhausting, frustrating, overwhelming and time-consuming. Make sure you are in agreement with the tasks given to you and don't allow them to make you unhappy and unfulfilled; don't forget you have a life and live your life with purpose; choose to focus on your tasks and accomplish them successfully.

Received

It is important how you are received by people. How you interact with people or how people interact with you is very important. I was told that some people tolerate other people, not really wanting that person(s) in their life, but since they are there, they will put up with a person to pass along time or if a person is helping another person, then they will tolerate him/her for what they need from that individual. Also, I was told, "be around people that celebrate you not tolerate you." Don't allow people that tolerate you, drain the life out of you, they will never appreciate you and your kindness. Enough said! Moving forward!

The Outside Me vs. the Inside Me:

Loving Me for Who I Am can be a little challenging! Due to the fact that we are not perfect! Due to the fact that we have flaws and issues, denotes that there are things in our lives we should acknowledge and deal with in order to have a sense of balance when we make decisions whether in relationships, jobs, friends, and family. This very thing that we struggle with is: The outside me vs. the inside me!

There is a real fight and/or struggle some women have within their inner-being. This fight and/or struggle is either physically, emotionally, mentally and/or spiritually, but it all comes from an inward struggle from hurting past and present events that has taken place in their lives. This fight is between the outside me vs. the inside me. The inside me is this timid, starved for attention, affection and love little girl. She wants the same attention that the outside me woman is receiving; whether it's from people, places or things.

The outside me lady makes sure she go to the spa for a body massage; she make sure she gets a manicure and pedicure; she make sure she go shopping for shoes, purses, clothes and perfume; she make sure she connect with friends, hang out and have a great time. Sometimes, women neglect nurturing, protecting, cultivating and inspiring that little girl on the inside of them and it leaves her open to be victimized by outside influences. This little girl inside of you is longing for affection, love, security and acceptance! She wants to be adorned! She wants to do things right, but she struggles with making right decisions vs. wrong decisions. Some women allow negative influences such as; people speaking negative words and negative behavior to filtrate their lives because they don't want to be alone and trying to please people in hopes of being accepted and not rejected. A hurting past can leave a lady devastated but she must protect herself from people's negative behavior, words and actions! Love and accept that little girl, give her the attention and love she desires and she will make you so happy and fulfilled in everything you do and the right people you allow to enter into your life will love you and accept you too!

The Outside Me:

There are many effects that can occur when a woman is fighting and/or struggling from a hurting past and present events that has taken place in her life such as: drug and alcohol abuse; unwed pregnancies; domestic violence; date rape; self-cutting; weight loss; weight gain; altering facial and body appearance; piercing; tattoos; poverty; crime; anger; suicide; rejection; poor grades; criticism; promiscuous behavior (sexually active); depression; sexual transmitted diseases; fear of failure; fear of success; disobedience to authority; oral sex; loved ones passed away; loneliness and parents' divorce. However, she should not camouflage it by going on a shopping spree or dancing the night away! She must find help to overcome her struggles!

The Inside Me:

There are many effects that can occur when a woman accepts, nurtures and love who she is; such as: living her life to the fullness; not allowing anyone to rob her of joy and purpose; she is able to embrace her peace, her passion, her uniqueness and love her creativity; she can treat herself to a shopping spree and not feel like she is fulfilling a void; she has the strength to avoid negative people and negative situations and she can conquer any task or situation with positive thoughts, words and actions! Love the new you!

Emotional Words and Definitions to Consider:

1. Nurture-anything that nourishes; food; upbringing; rearing;

2. Secure-free from danger; safe; free from doubt; stable; certain; to guard

3. Heal-to restore or return to health

4. Deliver-to be free; no longer bound.

5. Love-to feel love for; passion; heartfelt.

6. Protected-to keep from harm or injury; guard.

7. Appreciated-to value highly; to be thankful for

8. Supported-to hold up or in position; to provide with necessities; to defend

9. Encouraged-to impart bravery or confidence to; to give support to

10. Care-to be concerned or interested

11. Accepted-to receive willingly; to admit to a group or place

12. Insecure-unstable; shaky; lacking self-confidence

13. Loneliness-solitary (single); existing or alone

14. Bitterness-resentful; painful

15. Hopeless-lack of expectation; lack of energy

16. Help-to give relief to; aid; assistance

17. Disappointed-to fail to satisfy the hopes of; defeated

18. Unforgiveness-holding on the emotional hurts; difficult to let go of hurts; bitterness

19. Suicide-the act of intentionally killing oneself; one who commits suicide; no reason to live

These emotional words and definitions are therapeutic! They can help you recognize the downfalls in life and the success which can be gained with determination to overcome defeat! These negative words will control your life and will leave you missing out on great and wonderful things life has to offer! Avoiding negative emotions will not go away, it will remain in your thoughts and feelings until you are ready to deal with them! Setbacks, misfortunes and disappointments can affect your character, your prosperity and relationships. It has a tendency to make you stagnated and miss out on exploring and enjoying your life. Life has a way of teaching you how to grow up and refrain from being a victim of emotional damages. I encourage you not to allow these emotional thoughts and feelings control you any longer, now it's time to take back your love, your security, and protect and appreciate your amazing life; care and accept your happiness, peace and prosperity! You owe it to yourself! Live the wonderful life of acceptance and love!

Hurting words will leave hurting emotions; which develops from a lot of negative past and present experiences that has occurred in a person's life. How people deal with their emotions normally will affect how well they treat their bodies and it will determine how well their bodies treat them! A poor eating habit can cause the body not to function properly. Certain foods have the tendency to cause the body to be sluggish with the inability to perform daily routines.

However, eating healthy foods can energize the body, soul and mind! Healthy foods promote positive thinking! It promotes a healthy body inside and out! It promotes happiness! It promotes peace! It promotes healthy relationships! It eliminates mood changes and health problems! Dieting is not consistent! Eating healthy is life-changing! Every day, love the person you are! If you would like to make some changes, do so! It's your body! Below is a list of healthy food groups I found on WebMD website; I thought it would be helpful! Healthy foods you can eat and digest well!

WHOLE-WHEAT BREADS

MEAT AND SEAFOOD

- Skinless chicken and turkey breasts
- Ground turkey and chicken
- Salmon
- Reduced-sodium deli meats
- Tuna in water

PASTA AND RICE

- Brown rice
- Whole wheat pasta

OIL

- Extra virgin olive oil

CEREALS AND BREAKFAST FOODS

- Whole grain or multigrain cereals
- Oatmeal
- Whole grain cereal bars

SMOOTHIES

- Mixture of fruit and vegetables or just fruit

BEANS

- Kidney beans, black beans, split peas, lentils and garbanzo beans

DAIRY, CHEESE AND EGGS

- Skim milk, soy milk and low-fat milk
- Fat-free or low-fat yogurt
- Fat-free or low-fat cottage cheese
- Eggs or egg substitutes

SNACKS AND CRACKERS

- Whole grain crackers
- Dried fruit: apricots, figs, prunes, raisins, cranberries and blueberries
- Nuts: almonds, walnuts, peanuts, pecans and pistachios (roasted and unsalted)
- Seeds: sunflower seeds and sesame seeds
- Peanut butter, almond and soy butter
- Hummus

PRODUCE

- Fruit: bananas, apples, oranges, mangoes, strawberries, blueberries,
- Vegetables: sweet potatoes, baby spinach, broccoli and carrots

Loving Me For Who I Am!
The New and Improved You!!!!

AFFECTION!

You Mean The World To Me!

Care, Attachment, Closeness, Concern, Feeling, Kindness, Good-Will, Regard, Love, Endearment, Desire, Heart-Felt, Sentiment, Soft-Spot, Tenderness, Warmth

A Woman Wants Affection! You Mean The World To Me!

Every woman wants affection. It matters not how old she is, a lot of women desire and need affection! How does showing and receiving affection and make you feel? Affection is a natural emotion or feeling that automatically connects you to be close to another person. That desire is a drawing mechanism that says, "There is something about that person I like!" "I like the way she dress!" I like the way she smells!" "I am attracted to her intellect!" or "I like the way she carries herself!" There is an art to showing affection to the one you love. Affection will connect you to that special person in your life. Affection can be given to a person in different ways, it's not always a physical interaction with someone; there are many ways a person can express how much they care about another person and how much they need that person in their life: it can be a compliment, "you look beautiful today"; her gentle smile that brightens up the room when she walks in; or a pleasant conversation enquiring how was her day. Webster's dictionary defines affection as an attachment, to care and to desire. A woman wants affection: she would like someone who will be able to endure the highs and lows of life with her; she would like someone who is willing to love, show compassion and wholeheartedly and unconditionally give of themselves to her; and she would like for someone who will be able to embrace her happiness, peace and purpose. To make her feel special at all times!

How you feel will affect where you go in life; avoid allowing your negative emotions control your life! For years, I've had a desire to help hurting people, especially women. I often wondered why I would get upset when I saw or heard of a woman being physically abused; verbally insulted; emotionally damaged and mentally tormented by people she was in some kind of relationship with. Then one day, during a time when my feelings were hurt, the word "hurt" captivated my attention; I understood that women are emotional human beings. The wherewithal nature of a woman is to care, to love, to give, to nurture and to protect people she loves! Sad to say, but some people don't recognize her beautiful nature, they're only in her life to get what they want and need from her. Once they have used her up and she is drained from constantly giving and never being replenished then that person will disrespect, overlook and destroy her! Leaving her overwhelmingly feeling not appreciated.

People you allow in your life will affect your thoughts, your feelings, your behavior and your purpose positively or negatively. People can help you reach your destiny in life full of joy, happiness and success or they can hinder you from possessing your dreams, visions and desires with frustrations, discouragement and confusion. You have to be very careful who you allow in your life and be determined that you will not allow people to hinder you from reaching your goals. Don't get tricked and put high expectations on people meeting all your needs because it's impossible! Looking for affection in all the wrong places and people will not fill the need or void in your life. There are things you should consider: 1) how will people positively affect my life? 2) Do they possess the same aspirations in life as me? 3) Do they encourage me to reach beyond the limits and move forward? And 4) are they willing to sow their time, energy, financial resources and endurance to help me succeed in life? Find happiness within yourself! A man will not be able to fix everything wrong in your life; however, he can help you in areas he has knowledge and experience to alleviate some of pressure and stress you are carrying. People can only do what they can to help and support you. It is up to you to speak encouraging words and show yourself some affection! Go on, you deserve it!

What a person says and does has the ability to affect another person's life whether to succeed or fail. People you allow to enter into your heart should bring harmony into the relationship! What you say and do should show the depth of how much love and the affection you have for the one you love. Take inventory on what makes a woman happy by taking notes: what's her favorite color?, what's her favorite movie?, what's her birthday?, what's her favorite food?, what's her favorite perfume?, what's her favorite restaurant?, what makes her happy?, what makes her sad? And what upsets her? Your notes will help you to be able to effectively connect and give her the affection she desires! If you agree, every woman say, "Amen!" Affection has the power to see and embrace a person's gifts; motivate, cultivate and bring into fruition their purpose in life. Make sure people you hold most dear in your heart has the capabilities to connect with you to help you produce positive results. If not, they are wasting your time. Affection feels good, show her that she mean the world to you!

Annually, on February 14th which is Valentine's Day, the stores are crowded with people young and old purchasing chocolate candy, cards, bouquet of long-stemmed red roses, cuddling and cute teddy bears and making reservations at a nice restaurant weeks in advance or waiting 2-3 hours to be seated at an overbooked restaurant to celebrate their valentines; even children exchanged valentine cards with their classmates at school. Valentine's Day is one of the biggest and expensive holidays; people express their love to the one they love! I believe this expression of love should be shown throughout the year instead of a one day celebration. There may be women who do not have a man to take them out to eat or buy them flowers or chocolate candy; don't allow Valentines or not having a man in your life to celebrate this special holiday get you in a depressive mood; I encourage you to celebrate Valentine's Day by treating yourself to a nice meal, buy yourself some long-stemmed red roses, a cute cuddling teddy bear and some chocolate candy! Remember, a man only enhances your happiness, he doesn't make you happy! Celebrate you! When you do meet a very nice and distinguished gentleman, he will only continue what you have started! Agree?

Affection is an act of kindness! It is uplifting, supportive and courteous! It should be shown daily to people you love. It resonate care and comfort. It has the ability to let people know that you are important to them and you care about their well-being. Affection develops a strong companionship which brings you closer together, your needs are met, you recognize all the reasons why she is important to you and more quality time is spent together. People can show affection in many ways: a body massage, holding hands, prepare a warm bath, a hug, cuddling and communication. Being able to reach and touch another person alleviates tension (stress), depression and frustration. Be attentive to her needs and connect with her emotionally, give her the affection she needs and she will cherish the moment for a lifetime.

There are many special qualities of a woman that connects her to loving relationships! Her sensitivity, she has the ability to feel when you are hurting and will try to do what she can to help you through your challenging moment(s); her warmth, a loving feeling she has when you are successful and soaring high on a monumental occasion; her gentleness, she has the ability to embrace you while sharing words of encouragements to help you to stay focus on your dreams; her compassion, she know how to say the right words when you have made a mistake and not belittle you; she is a nurturer, she has the ability to bring healing and strength when you are feeling low or not feeling well; and she is a good listener, she doesn't interrupt you while you are talking and she has the ability to give you sound advice that will help you make right decisions. Her special qualities will bring balance, strength and endurance to the one who will embrace her qualities and apply them to their lives. When a woman show and give her time and love to you, she wants you to be successful in every area of your life and by all means the same love she gives to you, please give it to someone else. Love is unlimited!

Daily, in addition to your hectic schedule, take out some time and show affection to the woman you love because it will provide her with comfort and protection! In addition, it will enhance your relationship with care, happiness, support, trust, desire and kindness. Leave sticky notes on the wall, on the refrigerator, even on your pillow of poems to show her how much you appreciate her. Fill her ears and heart with the words, "I love you!" "I adore you!" and "I miss you!" Send her text messages and emails of pictures that says, "I'm thinking about you!" and "I appreciate you!" this will let her know how special she is to you.

Affection Feels Good!
Show Her And Tell Her How Much She Mean To You!

RESPECT!

Honored! I Will Do All I Can Not To Hurt You!

Admiration Given By Others, Account, Adoration, Courtesy, Dignity, Esteem, Consideration, Favor, Honor, Ovation, Recognition, High-Regard, Reverence, Tribute, Attention, Good, Valuable, Important, A Particular Way of Thinking About or Looking At Something

A Woman Wants To Be Respected! Honored! I Will Do All I Can Not To Hurt You!

The Golden Rule says, "Do unto others as you would have them do unto you."

Every woman wants to be respected. Respect goes along way! Respect begins and ends with you! Without respect, a person's character suffers. Webster's dictionary defines respect as a feeling of admiring someone or something that is good, valuable and important. It also says that respect should be treated in an appropriate way, in the way of thinking about or looking at something or someone. How do you feel about someone and how do you treat that person? We should value, admire, honor, appreciate and respect a woman's differences! Remember, she is unique; she is admired and highly regarded; fashioned to be that rare jewel that is beyond priceless!

For years, I have witnessed whether on television, music or in person, men and women degrading another woman's identity; her character! Men and women using such inhumane words relating to a female dog and a woman that earns her money illegally at night. I am amazed how some people think such language is intriguing! And it appears for some, they like it. It's funny! It's enough to witness men degrading a woman, but when women degrade each other, that's horrible! All the struggles and unfair treatments women had and still have to encounter; we as women should be able to speak well of each other whether you like her or not! Lastly, I've heard women degrade themselves; maybe she grew up being called degrading names from her parents or maybe she was in an abusive relationship(s) with an old fling. We live in the 21st century and it's sad that we still see and experience slave-like conditions. Such treatments enslaves a woman to a lifestyle that is not fit for a queen; the chains that bonds her to hear and live beneath who she was created to be! This should not be!

Respect is associated with your self-esteem. What is self-esteem? Self-esteem is how you think, feel and conduct yourself whether it's negative or positive or both. Also, it helps you to form your identity by defining who you are and explore your capabilities. To break down self-esteem: Self-is you, the whole you, your emotions, your feelings, your thoughts and your behaviors. Esteem is how you value and estimate your self-worth. If you reject or discard parts of your identity, you will destroy your self-worth and self-value. As an overall, women want to be loved, accepted, appreciated and valued by people who are important to them. A lot of people don't stop to find out what are their attributes? What do they like about themselves? When people see or hear them speak, what do people see or hear? What do they want to accomplish in their lives? What are their goals, dreams, visions or purpose? Take a moment to soul-search! What's keeping you from living your life full of happiness and freedom? How often do you compliment yourself, not in a conceited way? How many pats on the back do you give yourself? These questions can go on and on. I would like you to focus on positive or healthy self-esteem and come up with creative ways you can develop, enhance and maintain a positive or healthy self-image.

Some relationships fail due to a lack of respect! How you respect yourself and others will send signals on how you want to be treated and how you should treat other people! Due to the lack of respect and mistreatment in a relationship, there have been women who have attempt or succeeded with suicide! Sometimes, women in abusive relationships don't know what to do! You can't tell them to "just leave him" if she have been romantically involved with him; it's not that easy!

Women, we have to recognize the signs, when we see or hear another woman being abused in a relationship we should do what we can to help her! Don't talk about her, but try to help her! You might be her last hope!

Lack of respect can come from negative criticism or judgment on performances, appearances or successes from people who are very important in a person's life. Also, it comes from family dysfunctions (alcohol and drug abuse, lack of affection, critical comments and sexual abuse….); verbal, physical, mental and emotional abuse; depression; frustration and discouragement. Such feelings will leave scars of feeling unloved, worthless and hopeless. Consider this: every action, every decision or thought and every choice begins in your mind and it transmit that information to your heart and it ends with the results whether positive or negative, good or bad; the way we act is accordingly to what we think, say and do.

Respect, watch what it says and does! There is an old saying that says, "Sticks and stones may break my bones, but words will never hurt me." NOT TRUE! Negative (hurting) words have a way to crush you, devastate you and offend you! Sometimes, it can immobilize you from moving forward in life. I've learned that some people do not know how to talk to other people! Their people's skills are lacking in the compassionate department! It lacks in the understanding department! They haven't been acquainted with the self-sacrificing department! They don't consider how it makes you feel when they say hurting things. It's as if they don't care!

Respect never brings up a forgiven past; consistently reminding a person of what she used to do. She may smile on the outside and may agree with you that she did do it, but inwardly she still hurts, trying to get over her past mistakes. Making a mistake doesn't feel good and it has a way of sticking around when you want to move forward with your life, especially when you are trying to live a good life! When you allow people to walk over you, disrespect you and undermine you; you are showing weakness and a lack of confidence to them. You have to forgive yourself and/or forgive other people who have hurt you whether in your past or present or both and move forward! Please don't allow anyone to make you relive your past forgiven mistakes; they are the one who are stuck in the past and struggling to move forward in life, not you! Be confident with who you are and never allow anyone to disrespect you because you are someone special!

Respect will simply adore, love and appreciate people you love; it doesn't degrade, embarrass, offend and disrespect. Respect is honoring consistently giving due diligent to people you care about. It eradicates pettiness! It eradicated hurting and offensive words and actions! It eradicates controlling and belittling that person you love so much!

Respect has the capabilities to compromise! It's flexible with its time, energy and support! It respects people's time and space whether together or apart! It doesn't demand attention, throwing a temper tantrum in order to get its way and it doesn't manipulate or try to control someone's purpose! It has the capabilities to love and respect someone; love and respect never seeks to harm another. Rather, love and respect seeks peace, patience, forgiveness, understanding, wisdom, compassion and kindness.

Everyone doesn't think or act the same; treat her the way you would like to be treated! Honor her and she will honor you! Respect her and she will respect you!

One day while sitting in my car, I pondered the word respect and each letter was powerful! Here's what came to me:

Regain Efforts that Show Positive Energy and Character Towards yourself and others!

Now that's powerful! Right!

When we are in a relationship or just loving ourselves we must give and show respect! Let us not forget, if there is a lack of respect in a relationship, then there isn't a true and honest relationship; it's okay to admit when you have done or said something wrong; humble yourself, apologize and restore your relationship; true confession is good for the soul and your relationship! It's not important who's right and who's wrong all the time; we have to learn to let some things go and stop being so petty; we waste a lot of time and energy focusing and holding on to things that divides us from each other rather than focusing on the things that will enforce and strengthen our relationship. Some things are not that serious!

Respect forgives and forgets! It doesn't hold on for dear life the wrongs a person did or said! I'm not saying to allow people to keep hurting your feelings, or degrade you or disrespect you, but I am saying, remember, there were times when you weren't on your best behavior! There were times when you didn't say things sweetly to another person! There were times when you didn't think pure and kind thoughts about someone! The golden rule says, "Do unto others as you would have them to do unto you". We are not perfect, but when you can get out of self and start considering other's feelings, then you will be able to have strong relationships! It's sad when a person knowingly has hurt another person's feelings and their behavior is as if they never did or said anything wrong to hurt that person's feelings; they don't believe they need to apologize, they act indifferent with you as if you are the culprit and you need to be punished. Forgiving is a word that literally says, "I will not hold your wrong against you!" it also says, it's as if they have never did or said anything wrong to hurt you. Lastly, forgiving mean, "I free myself from all the negativity given by you!" Negative words! Hurt feelings! Bitter taste! Unforgiving heart is not worth being miserable because someone say or did something mean to you. I encourage you to "forget about it and move forward; it's their lost not yours!" If the relationship doesn't work, don't worry about; ONE WILL!

Remember, R-E-S-P-E-C-T Means!
Regain Efforts that Show Positive Energy and Character towards yourself and others!

Respect says, "I'm HONORED To Have You in My Life!

And I Will Do All I Can Not To Hurt You!

TRUST!

The Untold Secrets!

Strong Character, Strength, Truth, Integrity, Surety, Confidence, Firm Reliance, Commitment, Hope, Dependable, Loyal, Belief That Someone or Something is Reliable, Good, Honest and Effective, Ability, Trustworthiness, Faith, Trust

A Woman Wants Trust! The Untold Secrets!

Every woman wants trust. Trust is a word that requires confidentiality! It requires integrity! It requires commitment! It requires a strong character! It requires loyalty! It requires trustworthiness! Wow! I struggled a little with this word. Goodness! Everyone cannot be trusted! It doesn't matter how much sweet talking he/she says; all the unfulfilled promises made; with all the pretense emotions displayed and all the friendly enemies who entered and exited your life! To trust someone is not freely given, it takes time to trust someone you just met or have known for years, it's a process! And that process will not develop over night or in several days or years! Throughout some relationships, there will be a continuous trusting process, especially with people who have experienced mistrust in past relationships! When you have found someone that you can really trust, it will enhance and strengthen your relationship. Webster's dictionary defines trust as to a firm reliance, one committed to another person, having confidence placed in another, dependable and entrust. What makes a person trusting is having a good character! And having a good character makes a person trusting! When a person's character is above board; it has the capabilities to form a bond with another person. That bond is what connects and hold a relationship together! That bond will help you through the good times and the challenging times in your life! That bond will allow you to share personal and important information and you know that it will not be revealed to anyone!

The untold secrets! Secrets, which are confidential information; a woman will share her personal information with certain persons who will not divulge her business. She safeguards her life, her emotions, her feelings, her thoughts, her eyes and her ears! A woman is very selective when it comes to sharing her personal life with outsiders. She is not so readily to expose her deepest secrets! Her embarrassing moments! Her past or present nightmare relationships! Or her joyous, breathtaking and heart-throbbing relationship she has with the one she loves!

Trust develops after you made a promise to never share another person's untold secrets to anyone. It's very disheartening to find out what you have shared with someone is now being communicated by other people or someone talks about you to someone else and that person has a bad attitude and looks at you funny when you walk into a room and you haven't treated them badly.

Trust is willing to give up every heavy and disturbing emotional and draining experience from your past! Letting go everything and everyone who held you emotionally in bondage! Releasing fear, hate, isolation, regrets and setbacks! Look beyond and reach forward to your freedom, joy, dreams and peace that life can bring! Let go of people and things that are draining, complaining, moody and dream-killers!

I've found that a lot of women are hesitate to opening themselves up to receive another female into their life, some women reframe from sharing personal information about their relationships, job, money and successes because it's sad to say, but some women have the tendency to hate on another woman's prosperity! When they see their sister prosperous, it eats away at them and they began to say and do things to hurt them. Note: Never share personal information with someone you don't trust! If you do, you will be sorry! Trust me! I can write a book about it! Oh, I am! (Smile)

Listen! A woman wants a relationship that she feels she can trust the person she is sharing her most intimate and personal secrets with! She would like to be able to share her heartfelt thoughts and feelings! A woman can understand what another woman is going through! But she doesn't want her business exploited!

A woman wants a trusting, committed and lasting relationship! She wants to know if she can trust the special man in her life with her love! If she can trust him with her aspirations, her goals, her dreams, her visions and her passions! Can he be trusted with the love she has for him and that he doesn't break her heart! Use it and abuse it! She doesn't want to be in an untrusting relationship! She would like to know that special man will not promise her one thing and not fulfill his promise. Honesty is the best policy!

Below are some of the characteristics a woman should look for in a man, the pros and the cons! Make a list and see what outweighs the other (the pros or the cons); it will inform you if you will be able to trust him with your heart!

1. Does he love you unconditionally regardless of your body structure?

2. Does he support your dreams, visions and goals?

3. Does he listens, not just hear you when you are sharing your heartfelt feelings of hurt and disappointments?

4. Does he say, "I love you?" and "I appreciate you?"

5. Does he make you a priority? Are you at the top of his list?

6. Does he value your self-worth?

7. Does he embarrass you in front of people?

8. Does he criticize your appearance or dialect?

9. Does he buy things for himself and not you? Is he cheap?

10. Does he control you?

11. Does he wines like a little baby all the time?

12. Does he complains when things doesn't go his way?

13. Does he curse you out? Hit you? Or threatens you?

14. Does he suffer with low-esteem?

15. Does he disrespect you by looking at other women? Touching other women? Or consistently in other women's faces?

16. Does he lay around the house and not contribute to maintaining the home?

17. Does he rather hang out with the guys instead of spending time with you?

18. Does he communicate by texting you and not by calling you?

19. Does he acknowledge and celebrate special holidays or your anniversary or your birthdays?

20. Does he really know the really you?

Please, don't be afraid to accept certain people you want in your life! This is YOUR life and you make the decisions if you want to be loved or abused! If you want to be respected or disrespected! If you want to be free or in bondage! If you want to live a mediocre life or you want to live your life full of adventure and success! If you want to be low on someone priority list or on top of the list! The choice is YOURS! Trust the person you want to be and don't allow people to make you feel less than who you were created to be!

Trust celebrates a new and dawning beautiful day! This day allows you the opportunity to receive life's rewards! The rewards of new visions! New dreams! New aspirations! New goals! New purpose! New hopes! You are FREE! Free to be you! Free to trust again! Free to love again! Free to live again! Free to give again! Free from fear! Free from bondage! Free from stress! Live your best life now! You deserve the BEST!!!!

SECURITY!
Safety!!! Whew!

Safeguard, Free From Danger, Care, Anxiety or Doubt, Protection, Cover, Defend, Guard, Precaution, Promise, Guarantee, Retreat, Salvation, Shelter, Shield, Bond, Covenant, Redemption, Freedom from Fear, Surety, Freedom from Poverty or Want, Security

A Woman Wants Security! Safety!!! Whew!

Every woman wants security. Security, this word is huge! Webster's dictionary defines security as safety, something deposited as assurance of the fulfillment of an obligation and protected. Security provides freedom from danger, fear or anxiety. How many times have you been concerned about a situation not knowing which way to turn? What does the future hold for me? Will I be successful in life? We have been given the strength and courage to meet and accomplish our deepest desires! We don't give in to fear! We don't allow our situations to dictate to us! We are OVERCOMERS! There are a lot of women in this world, who have overcome struggles, disappointments, setbacks and poverty in their lives! They are women of power and of influence! They never allowed their circumstances hinder their future goals; they met their obstacles head on and defeated them! Today, many women are independent, professional and successful entrepreneurs, career builders, and have home-based businesses; they work and make their own money; they have the capabilities to maintain a very nice and comfortable living. These women own homes, drive nice cars, beautiful wardrobes in their walk-in closets and travel around the world. Yet, this can be quite challenging for the special man she has in her life. A man may feel that she doesn't need him because to him she has it all. But little does he know; a woman wants to feel safe from harm and danger; she wants to be able to let her guards down and have intimate conversations and know that special man in her life will not take advantage of her kindness, her money and her strength.

Some people look at the word security and think women want to be taken care of financially by a man. She wants his money, his car and his home, but a unique and distinguished woman is not gold-digger; she is well able to provide a great living for herself. If he is willing to share with her and she with him, together their home is established and prosperous!

Security has the ability to give fulfillment of life. It provides incentives to pursue endless possibilities, challenging situations and countless desires! It allows truth, peace, happiness and joy to set the tone of our confidence! Security provides protection! Security solves problems! It eradicates fear, failure, inadequacy and defeat! Security dictates how to live our lives with victory and success!

I've found out that the number one desire a woman wants is a hug! Outside of sex and money, a woman wants to be held, embraced, to feel secured, safe and protected! She wants to be loved, comforted, appreciated and understood! A hug is a skill and it has the tendency to send out signals of warmth, trust and passion! It's a beautiful feeling to be able to find comfort in the arms of a strong, confident, supportive, loving, gentle, happy, humorous and kind man! That lets her know that she is safe in his arms! His hug says, "I love you! I care about you! I need you! I respect you! I appreciate you! I support you! I will protect you!" That's so true!

Sometimes, a woman feels like the weight of the world is resting on her shoulders! She would love to be able to sit down at a quite restaurant or at home and talk to a seasoned, full of wisdom and a good listener man; who will understand how she feels and possibly provide her with sound advice that will help her with situation(s).

Security for a woman is being able to come home and know that her man got her back! If a woman is strong for everyone else then who can she be weak too? The woman is the backbone for her man; what will he be for her? She desires for her man to understand and support her endeavors! To be the strength she needs! She would like to know he is in her corner for moral support and comfort!

Vulnerability is a strong word and not so intriguing word for a woman! Some women feel being vulnerable makes her weak and needy, but the connotation of this word means more than that. I had a very interesting conversation with some great out-of-the-box thinking friends of mine and they enlighten me on the word vulnerability! One of my friends said, that being vulnerable allows a man to feel he is the strong one in the relationship! He is the protector! He ensures that the woman he loves is safe! He is the hunter! He will make sure if anyone hurt his woman, they will get hurt! Some men do not want to hoover over a woman! A lot of men aren't insecure in their relationships; he doesn't have to call her every five minutes to see where she is or follow her to ensure she is going where she said she was going or hire a private investigator to spy on her. A secure, hardworking, loving and trusting man doesn't have that kind of time; he is focused on providing a good living for his family, he is focused on loving his family unconditionally and protecting his family from all hurt, harm and danger.

Security allows you to breathe and know that your entire being and the people you love are safe! It allows you to know you do not have to fear of any violations from people who are out to destroy you! It allows you to be able to trust and love those who are close to your heart!

Security! Everything you need, desire and want can be found inside of you! Prosperity starts and ends with you! All your dreams and visions begin with you! Search your heart! Soul-search! What makes you happy? What makes you fulfilled! Dig it up! Write it down! Research it! Network with people who are doing what you want to do! Pray about it! Hang around positive purpose-driven people who are making a difference in your community, society and the world! People who are building businesses! People who are changing lives in your church! People who standing up for a cause! Don't limit yourself anymore! You can have the best in your life! You can be the best! You can live in the best neighborhoods! You can drive the best cars! You can have the best bank accounts! You can marry the best man! Whatever and whoever, you consider is the BEST, is the BEST for you!!!

Search your heart and pull out those awesome plans for your life! Live your best life NOW! Share with the world your awesomeness! Reap blessings! Reap divine favor!

Reap wealth! Reap success! Reap good and healthy relationships! Reap a happy and fulfilled marriage! Reap a healthy body! Reap beauty! Reap joy and peace! Reap WHAT A WOMAN WANTS!!!!

You Deserve The Best! Because You Are The Best!!!!!!

Endnotes

1. The Riverside Publishing Company, Webster's II New Riverside Pocket Dictionary Revised Edition

2. Author, La Presha L. Mastin, Searching The Inner Me Self-Esteem Manual, 2008

3. Seminar Message, La Presha L. Mastin, The Waiting Season 2014

4. Thomas Nelson, Inc., The Holy Bible King James Version, Reference Edition, 1989

5. Zondervan, King James and Amplified Versions Parallel Bible

6. Online Free Merriam-Webster Definition Dictionary

7. WebMD website, Healthy Foods

"Do You Know What Really Satisfies A Woman?"

What a woman wants encompasses more than what you may think! For centuries, people have tried to discover the intuition of a woman. A woman is one of the greatest creations that were ever made. We were fashioned (designed) to be unique, beautiful, wealth builders, kind, understanding and giving. Women are entrepreneurs, homemakers and career builders.

Phenomenal, you are! A woman has amazing characteristics that makes her unique. No one can do what she can do! She is the glue that keeps things together! She is the one that helps the universe evolve! She is the one to help bring peace to an unrest soul! Phenomenal! Phenomenal! That's who you are!

What A Woman Wants! In this powerful book, there are 7 areas of what a woman wants. A woman wants to be: 1) Loved; 2) Appreciated; 3) Accepted; 4) Affection; 5) Respect; 6) Trust and 7) Security. These seven areas are very important and they are associated to a woman's needs and desires. Discover the REAL woman and know what really satisfies a woman!

About The Author

La Presha La Valle Mastin is an author, motivator, founder and CEO of Searching The Inner Me Self-Esteem Manual; She is the founder and editor of "Celebrate The New You!" magazine and "Help! I'm Hurting!" newsletter created to help young people who are struggling with life's challenges.

"My responsibility is to be aware that people are in need of encouragement and support! It is my desire to help make a difference in the lives of people everywhere, to enlighten and to empower them to live their best life NOW; in turn, they will be able to enlighten and empower someone else!"

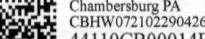
www.ingramcontent.com/pod-product-compliance
Lightning Source LLC
Chambersburg PA
CBHW072102290426
44110CB00014B/1789